Table of Contents

Projects

Techniques

Pink Tulip Quilt

Materials

Finished size 73½" (186.7cm) square

(This list includes enough materials to make the quilt as shown. If quilt size is altered, remember to calculate modified yardage requirements.)

10⅛ yds. (9.3m) white cotton batiste

3 yds. (2.7m) light pink cotton batiste

1½ yds. (1.4m) dark pink cotton batiste

3 yds. (2.7m) lightweight muslin for scrap

81" × 96" (205.7cm × 244cm) (full size) lightweight batting

Templates Required:

Inner Swag

Corner Swag

Small Flower Center Petal

Small Flower Petal

Small Flower Outer Petal

Large Flower Center Petal

Large Flower Petal

Large Flower Outer Petal

Large Flower Leaf

Large Flower Stem

Interlocking Hearts Quilting Template

General Supplies

(These are basic sewing room supplies that you may need while making blocks or during construction.)

White lightweight thread

Wash-a-way thread

Stabilizer

Wash-out marker

Temporary spray adhesive

No. 100 universal needle or no. 100 wing needle

No. 70 universal needle

Cutting

1. White batiste
   (cutting guide on page 28)

   a. Twenty-five 16" (40.5cm) squares for quilt top

   b. Two strips 3" × 208" (7.5cm × 528cm) for binding

   c. One 77" × 45" (196cm × 114.5cm) for quilt back

   d. Two 77" × 17" (196cm × 43cm) for quilt back

General Instructions

1. All seam allowances are ¼" (6mm) unless otherwise noted.

2. Do not cut appliqué pieces for pink appliqué motifs; refer to specific instructions to create appliqué pieces.

3. Specific techniques will be referenced in the instructions if needed.

4. Please read all instructions before beginning to stitch.

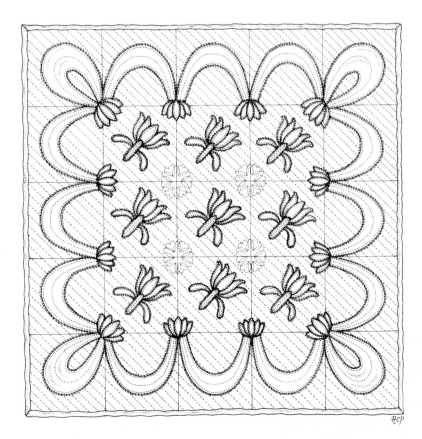

PIECED BLOCK BASE

1. Place two 16" (40.5cm) blocks right sides together and stitch one side using a ¼" (6mm) seam (fig. 1). Continue stitching 16" (40.5cm) blocks together until there are five blocks in a vertical row. Continue stitching blocks together to create five vertical rows of five blocks each (fig. 2). Press the seam allowances of each row in opposite directions, as shown in figure 2.

2. Place two rows of blocks right sides together, matching the seams. Pin and stitch using a ¼" (6mm) seam (fig. 3). Continue stitching the rows together until all five rows are joined to form the base for the Madeira Appliqué quilt top. Press well and set aside (fig. 4).

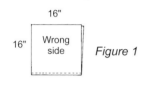

16"

16" Wrong side

Figure 1

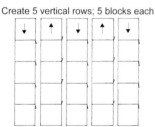

Create 5 vertical rows; 5 blocks each

Press seam allowances in opposite directions on alternate rows

Figure 2

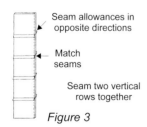

Seam allowances in opposite directions

Match seams

Seam two vertical rows together

Figure 3

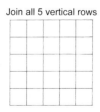

Join all 5 vertical rows

Figure 4

CREATING THE MADEIRA APPLIQUÉ PIECES

1. Two Madeira appliqué methods will be used to create the flowers and swags.

2. Create pieces for nine large flowers, twelve small flowers, four corner swags and twelve inner swags. Refer to each template for the color and the method of Madeira appliqué to be used for each piece. The solid lines on each template represent the sewing line. Do not stitch on the dashed lines.

Scrap Fabric Method

This method creates a shape with all or most of the edges turned under. Use it for the center flower petals, the stems of the flowers, the leaves and the swags; refer to the chart on page 6.

1. Place wash-a-way basting thread in the needle, bobbin or both. If the thread is used in either the needle or bobbin, lightweight thread can be used in the other.

2. Cut one square of fabric larger than the template in the desired color and one square of scrap fabric (muslin). Trace the pattern onto the wrong side of the muslin (fig. 5).

3. Place the two squares right sides together and stitch along the template solid line with a short, straight stitch (L=1.5). The dashed line (if there are any) of the template will not be stitched (fig. 6).

4. Trim the excess fabric ⅛" (3mm) to ¼" (6mm) from the stitching (fig. 7). Clip any curves or points (fig. 8).

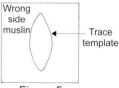

Wrong side muslin

Trace template

Figure 5

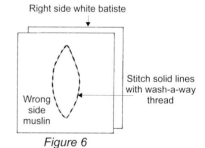

Right side white batiste

Wrong side muslin

Stitch solid lines with wash-a-way thread

Figure 6

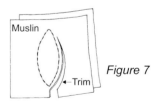

Muslin

Trim

Figure 7

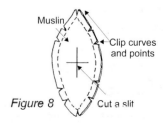

Muslin

Clip curves and points

Cut a slit

Figure 8

5. In the muslin, cut a slit large enough to easily turn the shape to the right side; see figure. Turn the shape to the right side through the opening. The seam allowance will be in between the two pieces. Using a wooden skewer, gently push out the points and curves. Press (fig. 9).

6. Starch lightly along the seams and press until dry. Gently pull the two pieces apart. If the two pieces do not pull apart easily, starch along the seam again and press until dry. Gently pull apart the two pieces creating one Madeira piece and one scrap piece. The scrap piece can be discarded (fig. 10).

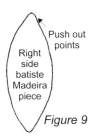

Push out points

Right side batiste Madeira piece

Figure 9

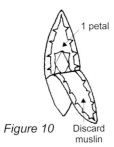

1 petal

Figure 10   Discard muslin

Mirror Image Method

This method creates two mirror image pieces at the same time. Use it when a part of the design does not have to be turned under. This method is needed for the light pink and dark pink outer flower petals of both the large and small flowers.

1. Place wash-a-way thread in the needle, bobbin or both. If the thread is used in the either the needle or bobbin, lightweight thread can be used in the other.

2. Cut two squares of fabric larger than the pattern in the desired color. Trace the pattern onto the wrong side of one square.

3. Place the two squares right sides together and stitch along the template solid line with a short, straight stitch (L=1.5). The dotted side of the template will not be stitched (fig. 11).

4. Trim the excess fabric ⅛" (3mm) to ¼" (6mm) from the stitching (fig. 12). Clip any curves or points (fig. 13).

5. Turn the shape to the right side through the opening. The seam allowance will be in between the two pieces. Using a wooden skewer, gently push out the points and curves. Press (fig. 14).

6. Starch lightly along the seams and press until dry. Gently pull the two pieces apart. If the two pieces do not pull apart easily, starch along the seam again and press until dry. Gently pull apart, creating two Madeira appliqué pieces that are mirror images of each other (fig. 15).

After all the Madeira appliqué pieces are completed, remove the wash-a-way thread from the sewing machine.

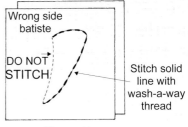

Wrong side batiste

DO NOT STITCH

Stitch solid line with wash-a-way thread

Figure 11

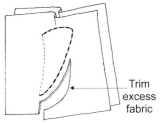

Trim excess fabric

Figure 12

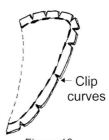

Clip curves

Figure 13

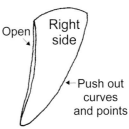

Open

Right side

Push out curves and points

Figure 14

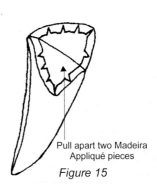

Pull apart two Madeira Appliqué pieces

Figure 15

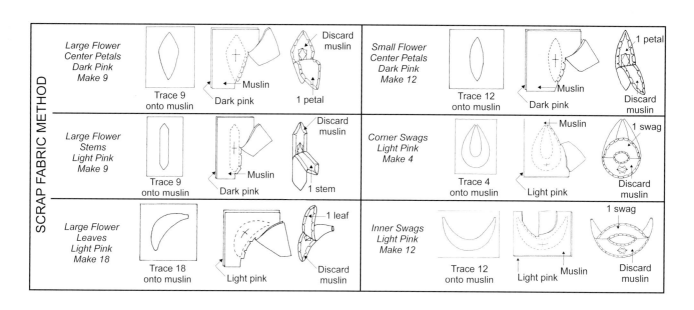

SCRAP FABRIC METHOD

Large Flower Center Petals Dark Pink Make 9
Trace 9 onto muslin — Muslin — Dark pink — Discard muslin — 1 petal

Large Flower Stems Light Pink Make 9
Trace 9 onto muslin — Muslin — Dark pink — Discard muslin — 1 stem

Large Flower Leaves Light Pink Make 18
Trace 18 onto muslin — Light pink — 1 leaf — Discard muslin

Small Flower Center Petals Dark Pink Make 12
Trace 12 onto muslin — Muslin — Dark pink — 1 petal — Discard muslin

Corner Swags Light Pink Make 4
Trace 4 onto muslin — Muslin — Light pink — 1 swag — Discard muslin

Inner Swags Light Pink Make 12
Trace 12 onto muslin — Light pink — Muslin — 1 swag — Discard muslin

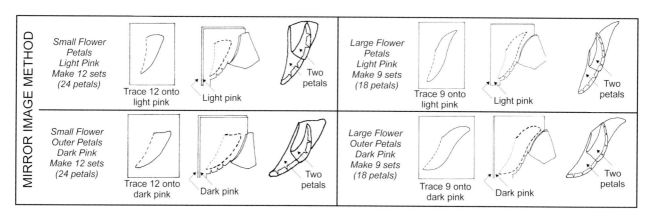

MIRROR IMAGE METHOD

Small Flower Petals Light Pink Make 12 sets (24 petals)
Trace 12 onto light pink — Light pink — Two petals

Small Flower Outer Petals Dark Pink Make 12 sets (24 petals)
Trace 12 onto dark pink — Dark pink — Two petals

Large Flower Petals Light Pink Make 9 sets (18 petals)
Trace 9 onto light pink — Light pink — Two petals

Large Flower Outer Petals Dark Pink Make 9 sets (18 petals)
Trace 9 onto dark pink — Dark pink — Two petals

Embellishing the Quilt Top

1. Using the templates, seam lines of the quilt top and the placement guide, trace all designs onto the quilt top using a fabric marker. Remember to trace the interlocking heart quilting template centered at each corner of the center block (fig. 16).

2. Spray the back of each Madeira appliqué piece with temporary spray adhesive. "Stick" the pieces to the quilt top in the correct location in the following order:

   Flower and swag border: swags no. 1, outer flower petal no. 2, flower petal no. 3 and center petal no. 4.

   Large flowers: outer petal no. 1, petal no. 2, center petal no. 3, leaves no. 4 and stem no. 5.

3. Stitching rules:
   Stitch the Madeira appliqué pieces in the order of placement; refer to step 2.

   If two pieces overlap each other, stitch along the edge of the top piece only.

   White lightweight thread is used for all stitching.

4. Using a no. 100 universal needle or no. 100 wing needle and a pin stitch, stitch the finished outer edge of each Madeira piece (see finished drawing). Stabilizer may be needed to prevent puckering. The straight side of the stitch will fall on the white fabric and the "fingers" of the stitch will catch the appliqué piece. Mirror image the stitch as needed to have the "fingers" catch the appliqué piece. If your machine does not have a pin stitch, use a regular needle and a small zigzag, blanket stitch or hemming stitch.

5. Trim 1¾" (4.5cm) from the outer edge of the quilt top. The squares on the outer edge should measure 14" (35.5cm) from the seam to the cut edge.

Completing the Quilt

(Refer to Applying a Continuous Binding in the technique section, page 25.)

1. To create the quilt back, stitch the narrower pieces (77" × 17" [196cm × 43cm]) to each side of the wider piece (77" × 45" [196 × 114.5cm]) with a ¼" (6mm) seam (fig. 17).

2. Layer and center as follows: quilt back (wrong side up), batting, quilt top (right side up).

3. Pin all layers together securely (fig. 18).

4. Quilt all layers together in the following order; refer to figures 18 and 19:

   1. Interlocking hearts

   2. Using a fabric marker and a ruler, mark a line corner to corner, diagonally across the quilt top. Quilt along the line stopping at each Madeira design or traced quilting design. Channel quilt in 1" (2.5cm) rows, stopping at each of the interlocking heart designs and at each Madeira design until the entire quilt is quilted (see finished drawing). For channel quilting, use a machine quilting bar as a guide or draw lines 1" (2.5cm) apart over entire quilt top.

   3. Quilt inside each swag ¼" (6mm) from each edge and the center.

   4. Quilt ¼" (6mm) from the edge of each petal and each leaf.

   5. Quilt the outline and in the center of each stem.

5. Trim all the edges of the quilt evenly.

6. Refer to the binding instructions in the technique section. Stitch the binding strips together to form one long piece. Fold in half and press to measure 1⅝" (4.1cm) in width. Attach the binding using a scant ½" (1.3cm) seam.

Trace all templates, seam lines and placement guides onto quilt top

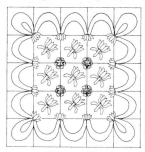

Figure 16

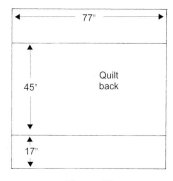

Figure 17

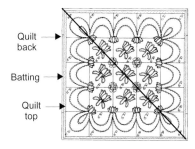

Figure 18

Quilting lines shown from wrong side

Figure 19

Blue Linen Quilt

MATERIALS

Finished size approximately 47" × 59" (119.5cm × 150cm)

This list includes enough materials to make a quilt with all blocks as shown. If you want to make a different size quilt, or if want to make a quilt using only one style of block, requirements for each block are listed with the instructions for that block, to allow you to figure yardage for your specific design. If quilt size is altered, remember to alter border pieces accordingly and calculate modified yardage requirements.

5¼ yds. (4.8m) blue linen, 60" (152.5cm) wide

(If you wish to use two colors: Blocks require 1½ yds. (1.4m; top and backing require 3¾ yds. [3.4m])

52" × 63" (132cm × 160cm) batting

9 yds. (8.2m) of 1⅛" (2.9cm) insertion lace

7 yds. (6.4m) of 1" (2.5cm) insertion lace

5 yds. (4.6m) of ⅝" (1.5cm) insertion lace

12 yds. (11m) of ¾" (2cm) lace edging

4½ yds. (4.1m) of ½" (1.3cm) lace edging

12 yds. (11m) of ⅞" (2.2cm) decorative ribbon

2½ yds. (2.3m) of 2" (5cm) blue organza ribbon

3 yds. (2.7m) entredeux

Ecru or off-white machine embroidery thread

Templates Required:

(located on pages 30-31)

Double Fans

Lace Insertion Heart

Mitered Lace Fan

Machine-Embroidered Diamond

Woven Lace Circle

Lace Weaving with Ruched Trim

Ruching Guide

Blue Linen Quilt Corner and Scallop

GENERAL SUPPLIES

(These are basic sewing room supplies that you will need while making blocks or during quilt construction.)

Optional: Open-toe appliqué foot

Optional: Edge-joining foot

Optional: Gathering or shirring foot

Optional: Walking foot or even-feed foot

1.6/70 twin needle and 7-groove pin tuck foot

No. 100 or no. 120 wing needle or universal needle

No. 80/12 or no. 90/14 universal machine needle

Tear-away stabilizer

Lace shaping board

Water-soluble fabric pen or pencil

Sewing thread to match linen for construction

Glass head pins

Safety pins or quilt-tack gun

Temporary spray adhesive or basting glue

CUTTING

1. Blue linen
   (pull threads for accuracy)

   a. Thirteen 12" (30.5cm) squares

   b. Two strips 3¼" × 24" (8.5cm × (61cm) for puffing

   c. Four strips 4½" × 12" (11.5cm × 30.5cm) for puffing borders

2. Blue organza ribbon

   a. Three pieces, each 17" (43cm) long

   b. Set aside remaining 1 yd. (91cm)

GENERAL INSTRUCTIONS

1. Linen will be easier to work with if each cut block is starched and pressed several times to give it body and crispness. (Do not starch two of the 8" (20.5cm) squares; they will be pin tucked and starch will make pin tucks flat.)

2. Specific techniques (if needed) are referenced in the instructions for each block.

3. All embellishment stitching is to be done with ecru or off-white machine embroidery thread in the universal needle unless otherwise noted. Construction will be stitched with regular sewing thread.

4. Adjust width and length for pin stitch, entredeux and baby daisy entredeux (optional), as desired, or refer to the chart on page 32. Work a practice piece to select the size, and write the settings here for later reference. When pin stitching, the straight part of the stitch is next to the lace heading on the fabric and the "fingers" of the stitch go into the lace heading. Entredeux stitches are centered over the lace headings.

5. Use the wing needle and tear-away stabilizer for all pin stitching and entredeux stitching. Remove stabilizer completely when stitching is finished. An open-toe appliqué foot makes it easier to follow the lace headings.

6. The edge-joining foot may be used when joining lace edges, and the walking or even-feed foot may be helpful during quilting.

Double Fans

Blocks 1, 4, 9 and 12

MATERIALS

BLOCKS NO. 1, NO. 4, NO. 9 AND NO. 12

(These amounts are for one block; for quilt as shown, make four blocks)

One 12" (30.5cm) square of blue linen

½ yd. (46cm) of 1⅛" (2.9cm) lace insertion

¾ yd. (69cm) of 1" (2.5cm) lace insertion

⅜ yd. (34cm) of ⅝" (1.5cm) lace insertion

1 yd. (91cm) of ¾" (2cm) lace edging

Ecru machine embroidery thread

Wing or large universal needle

Tear-away stabilizer

Template Required:

Double Fans

DIRECTIONS

(Refer to Lace Shaping on page 21.)

1. Trace the template onto two opposite corners of the block.

2. Place 1⅛" (2.9cm) insertion diagonally across the linen block and pin in place; refer to figure 1.

3. Shape and pin 1" (2.5cm) insertion along template lines A and C; shape and pin ⅝" (1.5cm) insertion along template line B (fig. 1). Refer to lace shaping instructions in the technique section.

4. Stabilize and pin stitch the inner and outer headings of insertions A and B, and the inner heading only of insertion C to the background block, using the wing needle and tear-away stabilizer; refer to figure 2.

5. Gather 18" (46cm) of ¾" (2cm) edging by pulling the top thread in the heading; adjust the length to fit the outer edge of insertion C and butt the heading of the edging to the outer edge of the insertion; pin in place. Using the wing needle and stabilizer, work entredeux stitch where gathered lace edging butts up to lace insertion C, catching the headings of both laces while attaching them to the background block (fig. 2).

6. Stitch a row of narrowed and shortened feather stitch (L=1.5; W=1.5) in each fabric space between the shaped lace insertions (fig. 3).

7. Carefully trim the fabric away from behind the lace insertions.

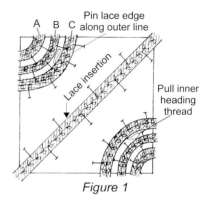

Figure 1

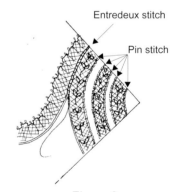

Figure 2

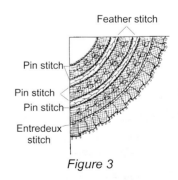

Figure 3

Lace Insertion Heart

Blocks 2 and 11

MATERIALS

BLOCKS NO. 2 AND NO. 11

(These amounts are for one block; for quilt as shown, make two blocks)

Two 12" (30.5cm) squares of blue linen

¾ yd. (69cm) of ⅝" (1.5cm) insertion lace

1½ yds. (1.4m) of ½" (1.3cm) lace edging

Ecru machine embroidery thread

Wing or large universal needle

Twin needle

7-groove pin tuck foot

Tear-away stabilizer

Template Required:

Lace Insertion Heart

DIRECTIONS

(Refer to Lace Shaping on page 21.)

1. Fold one 12" (30.5cm) linen block in half vertically and horizontally and press light finger creases to mark centers. Use the creases as centering guides to trace the heart template onto the block.

2. Shape and pin ⅝" (1.5cm) insertion around the traced heart. Refer to the lace shaping instructions in the technique section for shaping curves and miters.

3. Use the universal needle to stitch the outer edge only of the insertion to the fabric block with a narrow, open zigzag (W=1.5; L=1.0).

4. Trim the fabric away from inside the heart, very close to the zigzag; be very careful not to cut the stitches (fig. 1).

5. Cover the remaining 12" (30.5cm) unstarched blue linen square with double-needle pin tucks. Draw lines ½" (1.3cm) apart or use the edge of the pin tuck foot to space pin tucks instead of drawing lines. Stitch pin tucks with the double needle; refer to your specific machine instructions if help is needed.

6. Feather stitch in the spaces between pin tucks, using the same settings as for the Double Fans blocks (fig. 2).

7. Place the pin tucked square under the open-lace heart, centering a row of feather stitching or a pin tuck with the top and bottom miters of the heart (fig. 3).

8. Pin stitch the decorated fabric to the inside lace edge of the heart from the right side, using the wing needle and stabilizer. Remove the stabilizer and trim away the excess decorated fabric close to the stitching on the wrong side (fig. 4).

9. Gather the ½" (1.3cm) edging by pulling the top heading thread; adjust the length to fit the outer edge of the heart. Butt the headings together and attach to the linen block with the entredeux stitch, using the wing needle and stabilizer with the same technique used for the Double Fans blocks; refer to the finished drawing. Turn the raw ends under when beginning and ending.

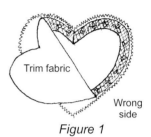

Trim fabric

Wrong side

Figure 1

Pin tucks Feather stitch

Figure 2

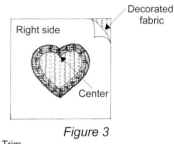

Decorated fabric

Right side

Center

Figure 3

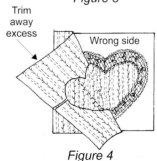

Trim away excess

Wrong side

Figure 4

11

Mitered Lace Fan

Block 3

MATERIALS

BLOCKS NO. 3

One 12" (30.5cm) square of blue linen

¾ yd. (69cm) of 1" (2.5cm) insertion lace

¾ yd. (69cm) of ¾" (2cm) lace edging

1 yd. (91cm) blue organza ribbon

Ecru machine embroidery thread

Wing or large universal needle

Tear-away stabilizer

Template Required:

Mitered Lace Fan

DIRECTIONS

(Refer to Lace Shaping on page 21.)

1. Fold the 12" (30cm) linen block in half vertically and horizontally and press light finger creases to mark centers. Using the creases as centering guides, trace the fan template onto the block.

2. Using the wing needle and stabilizer, work an entredeux stitch or baby daisy stitch along the spoke lines inside the fan (fig. 1). Stitch a practice piece to determine settings or refer to the chart on page 32.

3. Shape 1" (2.5cm) insertion across the top points of the fan, mitering the lace at the inner and outer points according to the instructions in the technique section (fig. 1). Use the wing needle and stabilizer to pin stitch along both headings of the insertion.

4. Gather the ¾" (2cm) lace edging by pulling the top heading thread. Adjust the length to fit the bottom of the fan and pin the lace in place, making sure that the ends of the insertion lace are covered. Adjust the gathers to allow more fullness at the lower point to prevent cupping at the bottom of the fan. Turn the raw edges under at each end.

5. Attach the heading of the gathered lace with the same stitch used on the inner spoke lines (fig. 2).

6. Remove the stabilizer and trim the fabric away from behind the insertion lace.

7. Tack the center of the organza ribbon to the bottom point of the fan. Tie a bow with loops about 3½" (9cm) long. Trim the tails of the bow to about 4" (10cm) long.

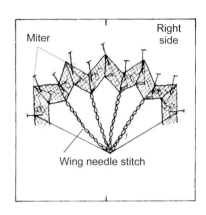

Figure 1

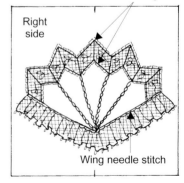

Figure 2

Puffing and Lace Strips

Blocks 5 and 8

MATERIALS

BLOCKS NO. 5 AND NO. 8

(These amounts are for one block; for quilt as shown, make two blocks)

One linen strip 3¼" × 24" (8.5cm × 61cm)

Two linen strips 4½" × 12" (11.5cm × 30.5cm)

52" (132cm) entredeux

26" (66cm) of 1⅛" (2.9cm) insertion lace

Ecru machine embroidery thread

Optional: gathering or shirring foot

DIRECTIONS

(Refer to Gathering Foot Puffing on page 24 and Beginning French Sewing techniques on page 20.)

1. Use the long linen strip to make puffing according to the instructions in the technique section. Slightly loosen the needle tension and run two rows of gathering stitches ¼" (6mm) and ⅝" (1.5cm) from each long edge. A gathering or shirring foot can be used; refer to the specific machine instructions if help is needed.

2. Pull the bobbin threads and gather the strip to measure 12" (30.5cm), or adjust shirred strip as needed (fig. 1).

3. Cut the entredeux into four pieces, and cut the insertion lace into two pieces. Attach entredeux to both edges of each lace piece; refer to Beginning French Sewing on page 20 (fig. 2).

4. Attach one lace/entredeux strip to each edge of the puffing strip (fig. 2).

5. Stitch the remaining two fabric strips to each entredeux edge of the puffing strip (fig. 2).

6. Trim the block to 12" (30.5cm) square, keeping the puffing strip centered.

Puffing strip gathered to 12"

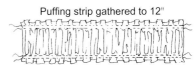

Figure 1

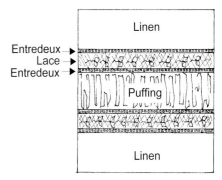

Figure 2

Machine-Embroidered Diamond

Block 6

MATERIALS

BLOCK NO. 6

Two 12" (30.5cm) squares of blue linen

⅞ yd. (80cm) of 1" (2.5cm) insertion lace

1½ yds. (1.4m) of ½" (1.3cm) edging lace

⅞ yd. (80cm) of ⅝" (1.5cm) insertion lace

Ecru machine embroidery thread

Wing or large universal needle

Tear-away stabilizer

Stabilizer for machine embroidery

Optional: Stranded cotton embroidery floss, ecru

Template Required:

Machine-Embroidered Diamond

Optional hand embroidery template or machine embroidery design approximately 3½" (9cm) to 4" (10cm) square

DIRECTIONS

(Refer to Lace Shaping on page 21.)

1. Fold one 12" (30.5cm) linen block in half vertically and horizontally and finger press lightly to crease and mark the center. Align the center template lines onto the center marks on the fabric. Trace all lines from the template onto the linen block.

2. Shape 1" (2.5cm) lace insertion along the curved template lines in each corner. Pin stitch the inner headings only to the fabric block.

3. Cut the edging lace into four pieces. Gather a piece of edging to fit the outer edge of the curved lace in each corner. Pin the edging to the fabric block, butting the headings together. Using the wing needle and stabilizer, stitch both headings to the block with entredeux stitch using the same technique as for the Double Fans blocks.

4. Shape the center diamond using ⅝" (1.5cm) lace insertion, mitering corners according to the directions in the technique section. Stabilize and pin stitch the outer edge only of the diamond and cut away the fabric from inside the diamond, carefully trimming close to stitches (fig. 1).

5. Using stabilizer, stitch an embroidered bow centered on the remaining 12" (30.5cm) blue linen square. Use the optional bow template to embroider by hand, or choose a machine embroidery design and use stabilizer.

6. Center the embroidered piece under the open diamond and pin in place. Stabilize and pin stitch the inner lace edge of the diamond to the embroidered piece (fig.2).

7. From the wrong side, remove the stabilizer and trim the excess embroidered fabric close to the pin stitching without cutting the stitches (fig. 3).

8. Trim the fabric from behind the corner lace insertions.

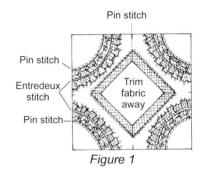

Figure 1

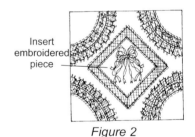

Figure 2

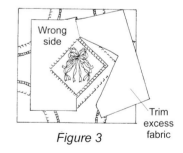

Figure 3

Woven Lace Circle

Block 7

MATERIALS

BLOCK NO. 7

One 12" (30.5cm) square of blue linen

1¼ yds. (1.1m) of 1" (2.5cm) insertion lace

⅞ yd. (80cm) of ⅝" (1.5cm) insertion lace

1⅝ yds. (1.5m) of ¾" (2cm) lace edging

Ecru machine embroidery thread

Wing or large universal needle

Tear-away stabilizer

Template Required:

Woven Lace Circle

DIRECTIONS

(Refer to Lace Shaping on page 21.)

1. Fold the 12" (30.5cm) linen block in half vertically and horizontally and finger press lightly to crease and mark the center. Align the center template lines onto the center marks on the fabric. Trace all lines from the template onto the linen block.

2. Cut the 1" (2.5cm) insertion into six 7½" (19cm) pieces. Place the lace over the design lines inside the circle and pin one end. Weave the lace in and over-and-under pattern according to the diagram and pin in place; refer to figure 1.

3. Shape ⅝" (1.5cm) lace insertion around the circle outline using the instructions in the technique section for shaping curves. Pin the outer heading along the design line; only the inner edge of this insertion should cover the ends of the woven insertion laces. Overlap the raw ends and turn under the upper lace end. Trim the woven laces if necessary so that the ends are covered by the circle of insertion and do not extend past the design line (fig. 1).

4. Use the wing needle and stabilizer to pin stitch both sides of all of the woven insertions. Pay attention to the weave of the lace. Stop where the lace goes under another piece and jump over to the other side; stitch only the lace that crosses on top. Also pin stitch the inner edge only of the circle (fig. 2).

5. Gather the ¾" (2cm) lace edging to fit the circle outer edge. Pin the gathered edging to the block with headings butted together the same as the Double Fans blocks. Turn the raw ends under. Using the wing needle and stabilizer, select the baby daisy entredeux stitch to attach the headings to the block (fig. 3).

6. Remove the stabilizer and trim the fabric from behind the circle of lace insertion.

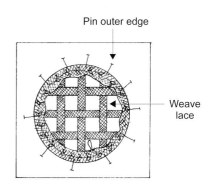

Figure 1

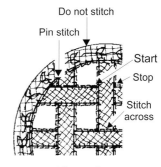

Figure 2

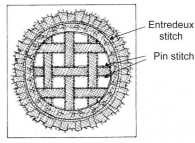

Figure 3

Lace Weaving
with Ruched Trim
Block 10

MATERIALS

BLOCK NO. 10

One 12" (30.5cm) square of blue linen

⅞ yd. (80cm) of 1" (2.5cm) insertion lace

⅝ yd. (57.2cm) of ⅝" (1.5cm) insertion lace

Three 17" (43cm) pieces of blue organza ribbon

Ecru machine embroidery thread

Wing or large universal needle

Tear-away stabilizer

Template Required:

Lace Weaving with Ruched Trim Ruching Guide

DIRECTIONS

1. Fold the 12" (30.5cm) linen block in half vertically and horizontally and finger press lightly to crease and mark the center. Align the center template lines onto the center marks on the fabric. Trace all lines from the template onto the linen block.

2. Cut the 1" (2.5cm) insertion into four 7" (18cm) pieces. Place the insertion strips over the design lines in the center of the template. Pin one end of each piece and weave in an over-and-under pattern as indicated in figure 1; pin in place. Turn under the top edge of each lace strip to create a finished edge at the top (fig. 1).

3. Shape ⅝" (1.5cm) lace insertion along the side and bottom edges of the design, mitering corners according to the instructions in the technique section. Turn the edges under to create a finished edge at the top as before.

4. Use the wing needle and stabilizer to pin stitch both sides of all insertions. Pay attention to the crossings of the woven lace as for the Woven Lace Circle block. Stitch only the lace that crosses on top (fig. 4).

5. Transfer markings from the ruching guide onto one organza ribbon piece. Work running stitch along the marked lines and pull up the strip to measure 6" (15cm) (fig. 2). Hand stitch the ruched ribbon in place across the top edge of the crest.

6. Make a rosette from each remaining piece of organza ribbon. Stitch the short ends together to form a circle; by hand, work a running stitch ½" (1.3cm) from one edge. Pull up the gathering thread tightly to gather the rosette and secure with stitches in the center (fig. 3). By hand, stitch a rosette at each end of the ruched ribbon (fig. 4).

7. Trim the fabric away from behind the outer lace insertion.

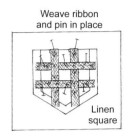

Weave ribbon and pin in place

Linen square

Figure 1

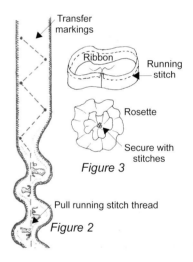

Transfer markings

Ribbon

Running stitch

Rosette

Secure with stitches

Figure 3

Pull running stitch thread

Figure 2

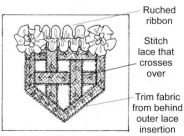

Ruched ribbon

Stitch lace that crosses over

Trim fabric from behind outer lace insertion

Figure 4

Constructing the Quilt

MATERIALS

3¾ yds. (3.4m) blue linen, 60" (152.5cm) wide

One piece batting, 52" × 63" (132cm × 160cm)

12 yds. (11m) of ⅞" (2.2cm) decorative ribbon

6 yds. (5.5m) of 1⅛" (2.9cm) insertion lace

6 yds. (5.5m) of ¾" (2cm) lace edging

Construction thread to match linen

Machine embroidery thread to blend with decorative ribbon

Template Required:

Blue Linen Corner and Scallop

CUTTING

1. Blue linen
(pull threads for accuracy)

  a. One quilt top, 52" × 63" (132cm × 160cm)

  b. One quilt back, 52" × 63" (132cm × 160cm)

2. Decorative ribbon

  a. Three 36" (91.5cm) strips

  b. Two 48" (122cm) strips

QUILT TOP ASSEMBLY

1. After completing all blocks, rinse to remove markings if needed. Lightly spray starch and press dry, being careful not to flatten gathered laces.

2. Lightly starch and press the 52" × 63" (132cm × 160cm) quilt top fabric piece. Fold and mark vertical and horizontal centers on the right side of the fabric.

3. Place the quilt top fabric piece onto a large, flat surface, right side up. Be careful in handling, keeping the fabric on grain vertically and horizontally.

4. Position the blocks onto the quilt top piece according to figure 1. Begin with the center blocks and work out, using the vertical and horizontal center lines as guides. Pin or glue-baste each block in place. The edges of the blocks should just touch, not overlap.

5. Use the three 36" (91.5cm) strips of decorative ribbon to run between horizontal rows of blocks. Center each ribbon strip over the joined edges of the blocks (half of the ribbon width should be on each block). Pin or glue-baste each ribbon in place; refer to figure 1.

6. Use a narrow, open zigzag to stitch along all ribbon edges through all layers. The zigzag should be wide enough to catch the entire ribbon heading and about 1.5mm (a little less than ¹⁄₁₆") long. Use a regular zigzag foot, edge-joining foot or open-toe appliqué foot. Use a machine embroidery thread color that will not be highly visible.

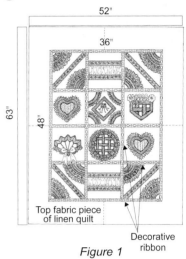

Figure 1

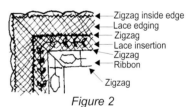

Miter all corners

Zigzag inside edge
Lace edging
Zigzag
Lace insertion
Zigzag
Ribbon
Zigzag

Figure 2

Zigzag inside scalloped edge of lace edging

Figure 3

7. Use the 48" (122cm) strips of decorative ribbon between vertical columns. Center and stitch the ribbons in the same manner as for the horizontal rows; refer to figure 1.

8. Frame the center blocks with the remaining decorative ribbon. Center the ribbon over the block edges as before; start in one corner and miter all corners. Pin or glue-baste in place (fig. 1).

9. Repeat step 8 on the outside ribbons with lace insertion, butting the inside edge of the insertion next to the ribbon edge. Repeat with lace edging, butting the straight edge of the edging to the outer edge of the insertion lace. Miter all lace corners; refer to figure 2. Refer to Lace Shaping on page 21.

10. Stitch all edges as before with a narrow, open zigzag; also stitch the outer edge of the lace edging. Keep the zigzag entirely on the lace near the scalloped edge so the stitches do not show on the fabric (figs. 2 and 3).

FINAL ASSEMBLY

NOTE: Construction seam will be stitched on traced line, then trimmed to ¼" (6mm).

1. Trace the quilt corner and scallop template onto the wrong side of the quilt top. Place the inner points of the scallops 2½" (6.5cm) from the outermost zigzag line; refer to figure 4.

2. Place the batting onto a large, flat surface. Place the quilt backing right side up over the batting. Place the quilt top right side down over the quilt backing, matching raw edges (fig. 4). Pin or tack well through all layers.

3. Straight stitch (L=2.5) on the traced scallop line, leaving an opening for turning. Stitch again with shortened stitch (L=2.0).

4. Trim the seam allowance to ¼" (6mm). Clip the inner points and grade seam allowances as necessary.

5. Slip your hand between the quilt front and back and turn the quilt right side out; the batting should be between the two fabric layers. Turn the corners carefully. Press the outer edges flat and hand stitch the opening closed.

6. Topstitch ¼" (6mm) from the outer edge (fig. 5). If available, a walking foot is very helpful for this step.

7. Baste all layers together by hand, by machine, with safety pins or a tack gun.

8. Quilt with straight stitch in the ditch along all ribbon and lace edges, inside all blocks as well as around the "frame" (fig. 6).

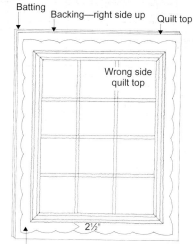

Template traced onto wrong side of quilt top
Figure 4

Figure 5

Figure 6

18

Beginning French Sewing

LACE TO LACE

Butt together and zigzag.

Suggested machine settings:
Width 2½, Length 1.

LACE TO FABRIC

Place right sides together.

Fabric extends ⅛" (3mm) from lace.

Zigzag off the edge and over the heading of the lace.

Suggested Machine Settings: Width 3½, Length ½ to 1 (almost a satin stitch).

LACE TO ENTREDEUX

Trim batiste from one side of the entredeux.

Butt lace to entredeux and zigzag.

Suggested Machine Settings: Width 2½, Length 1½.

GATHERED LACE TO ENTREDEUX

Trim one side of the entredeux.

Gather lace by pulling heading thread.

Butt together and zigzag.

Suggested Machine Settings: Width 2½, Length 1½.

ENTREDEUX TO FLAT FABRIC

Place fabric to entredeux, right sides together.

Stitch in the ditch with a regular straight stitch.

Trim seam allowance to ⅛" (3mm).

Zigzag over the seam allowance.

Suggested Machine Settings: Width 2½, Length 1½.

ENTREDEUX TO GATHERED FABRIC

Gather fabric using two gathering rows.

Place gathered fabric to entredeux, right sides together.

Stitch in the ditch with a regular straight stitch.

Stitch again 1/16" (2mm) away from the first stitching.

Trim seam allowance to ⅛" (3mm).

Zigzag over the seam allowance.

Suggested Machine Settings: Width 2½, Length 1½.

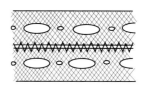

Lace to Lace

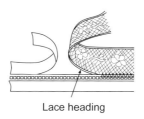

Lace to Entredeux

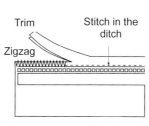

Entredeux to Flat Fabric

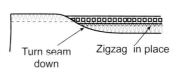

Topstitch

OPTIONAL: TOPSTITCH
(to be used after Entredeux to Flat or Gathered Fabric)

Turn seam down, away from the lace, entredeux, etc.

Tack in place using a zigzag.

Suggested Machine Settings: Width 1½, Length 1½.

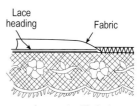

Lace to Fabric

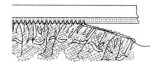

Gathered Lace to Entredeux

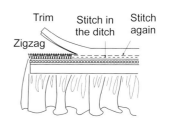

Entredeux to Gathered Fabric

Lace Shaping

CURVES, MITERS, HEARTS, OVALS AND DIAMONDS

1. Trace the lace shape and miter lines onto the fabric with a wash-out pen or pencil (see fig. 1). Place the fabric on a padded surface, such as a lace shaping board or ironing board. Note: If only one line is given for the template, shape the lace on the inside of the template. For scallops, shape the lace above the curve as shown in fig. 1. Scallops contain both curves and fold-back miters and are used in the illustrations.

2. To shape a curve, place the outer edge of the lace along the outer template line. Pin the lace to the template line by pushing glass head pins through the lace and fabric at an angle, into the padded surface. (Do not use plastic head pins because they will melt.) Pin only along the outer edge; the inner edge will be loose and curvy (see fig. 1).

3. To miter, let the lace extend past the point (miter line) in a straight line. Pin the lace to the miter line at points A and B (fig. 1).

4. Fold the extended end of the lace on top of itself. Leave the pin at B just as it is; remove the pin at A and re-place it through both layers (fig. 2).

5. Continue to guide the lace along the next section of the template. Pin along the outer lace edge as before (fig. 3). Note: If part of the folded miter peeks out, just push it underneath the lace; it can be trimmed away later.

6. To shape the inner edge, slip the point of a pin under the top heading thread of the lace at the point of the miter, or at the center of a section between the miters; refer to the illustration for gathered lace. Pull the heading thread just until the lace is flat against the fabric (fig. 4)

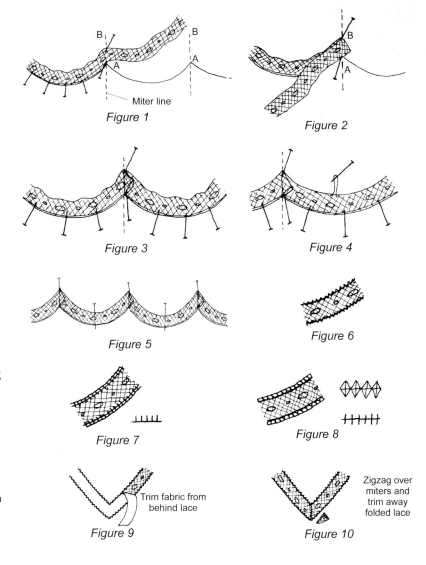

Figure 1
Miter line

Figure 2

Figure 3

Figure 4

Figure 5

Figure 6

Figure 7

Figure 8

Figure 9
Trim fabric from behind lace

Figure 10
Zigzag over miters and trim away folded lace

7. Lightly starch and press as each section is shaped or after the entire design is pinned. The iron can be placed directly over the glass head pins; press until dry. Remove the pins and pin flat through the lace and fabric only, removing it from the padded surface (fig. 5).

8. Stitch the lace edge(s) to the fabric using one of the following methods. Note: The specific directions will indicate if one edge or both edges of the lace are to be stitched.

• small zigzag (L=0.5–1.0, W=1.5–2.0) (fig. 6)

• place tear-away stabilizer behind the design, use a large needle or wing needle and pin stitch (L=2.0–2.5, W=1.5–2.0). The straight side of the stitch should fall on the fabric while the "fingers" of the stitch will catch the lace (fig. 7)

• place tear-away stabilizer behind the design, use a large needle or wing needle and an entredeux stitch (fig. 8)

9. Carefully trim the fabric from behind the lace, close to the stitching (fig. 9). Stitch along the lace miters with a small zigzag and trim the excess lace at the miters (fig. 10).

10. *To shape an oval or circle*—Pin in the outer edge of the lace along the template line. Overlap the ends of the lace by 1" (2.5cm). Pull the heading threads along the inner edge of the lace (refer to step 6). Fold the top piece of lace under ½" (1.3cm) (fig. 11). Lightly starch and press the oval and pin the lace to the fabric only (refer to step 7). Stitch as directed in the instructions (refer to step 8). See the illustrated steps on page 23.

11. *To shape a diamond*—Place the lace inside the template with the outer edge of the lace along the template line. Allow the end of the lace to extend beyond the lower point placing pins at A and

B (fig. 12). Continue mitering at each point (refer to step 3). When returning to the lower point, use the fold back miter method as follows: Crisscross the ends of the lace at the miter line. Place pins through both layers of lace at B (fig. 13). Remove the pin at A and fold the tail of the upper lace under to lie directly on top of the beginning lace tail. Repin at A (fig. 14). Lightly starch and press the diamond and pin the lace to the fabric only (refer to step 7). Stitch as directed in the instructions (refer to step 8). Carefully trim the fabric from behind the lace (refer to fig. 9). Stitch along the lace miters with a small zigzag and trim the excess lace at the miters (refer to fig. 10). Figure 15 shows the lace diamond stitched to the fabric using a zigzag stitch. See the illustrated steps on page 23.

12. *To shape a heart*—Begin at the lower point (A). Pin the outer edge of the lace along one side of the heart template. Miter at the inner point (refer to steps 3-5). Pin the lace along the remaining curve. Pull the heading threads along the inner edge of the lace (refer to step 6) (fig. 16). Lightly starch and press the heart and pin the lace to the fabric only (refer to step 7). Stitch as directed in the instructions (refer to step 8). Carefully trim the fabric from behind the lace (refer to fig. 9). Stitch along the lace miters with a small zigzag and trim the excess lace at the miters (refer to fig. 10). See the illustrated steps on page 23.

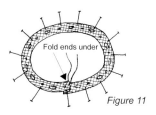

Fold ends under

Figure 11

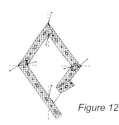

Figure 12

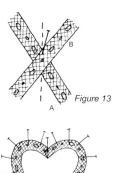

Figure 13

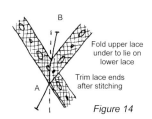

B

Fold upper lace under to lie on lower lace

Trim lace ends after stitching

A

Figure 14

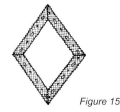

Figure 15

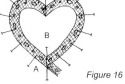

B

A

Figure 16

Tied Lace Bows

1. Tie 1 to 1¼ yards (91cm to 114cm) of lace insertion, edging, or beading into a bow, leaving equal streamers on either side of the bow.

2. Using a lace board, shape the bow onto the fabric according to the instructions on page 21.

3. Shape the streamers of the bow according to the instructions on page 21.

4. Fold the ends of the streamer into an angle.

5. Zigzag or machine entredeux stitch the shaped bow and streamers to the garment.

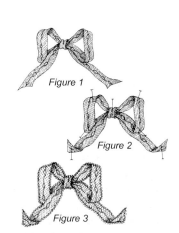

Figure 1

Figure 2

Figure 3

Hearts

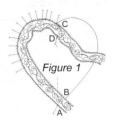

Figure 1

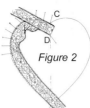

Figure 2

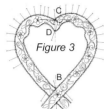

Figure 3

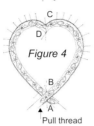

Figure 4
Pull thread

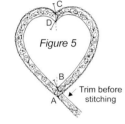

Figure 5
Trim before stitching

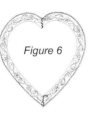

Figure 6

Circles

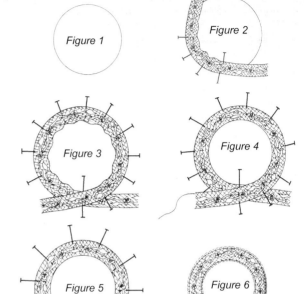

Figure 1

Figure 2

Figure 3

Figure 4

Figure 5

Figure 6

Diamonds

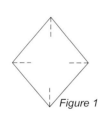

Figure 1

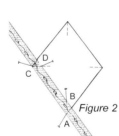

Figure 2

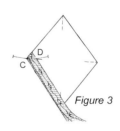

Figure 3

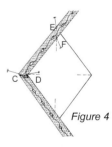

Figure 4

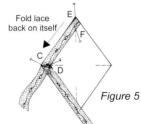

Fold lace back on itself

Figure 5

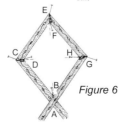

Figure 6

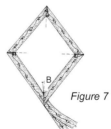

Figure 7

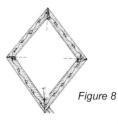

Figure 8

Gathering Foot Puffing

1. The speed of the sewing needs to be consistent. Sew either fast or slow but do not sew fast then slow then fast again. For the beginner, touch the "sew slow" button (if available on your machine). This will help to keep a constant speed.

2. The puffing strip should be gathered with a ½" (1.3cm) seam allowance, with an approximate straight stitch length of 4, right side up (fig. 1). Remember that you can adjust your stitch length to make your puffing looser or fuller. Do not let the strings of the fabric wrap around the foot of the machine. This will cause the fabric to back up behind the foot and create an uneven seam allowance, as well as uneven gathers. Leave the thread tails long in case adjustments are needed. One side of the gathering is now complete (fig. 2).

3. Begin gathering the second side of the strip, right side up. This row of gathering will be made from the bottom of the strip to the top of the strip. In other words, bi-directional sewing (first side sewn from the top to the bottom, second side sewn from the bottom to the top) is allowed. Gently unfold the ruffle with the left hand allowing flat fabric to feed under the foot. Do not apply any pressure to the fabric (fig. 3). The feeding must remain constant. Leave the thread tails long in case adjustments are needed. The puffing strip is now complete.

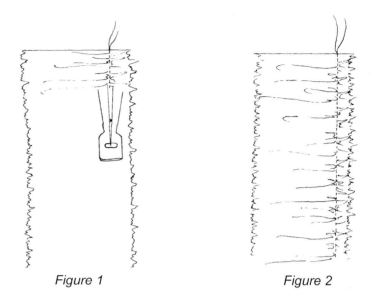

Figure 1   Figure 2

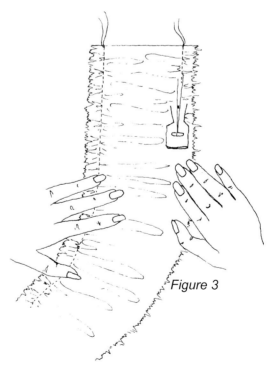

Figure 3

Applying a Continuous Binding

1. Cut fabric strips for the binding as directed in the project instructions. Place two strips right sides together. Stitch the layers together with a diagonal seam (fig. 1).

2. Trim the excess fabric ¼" (6mm) beyond the stitched seam. Press the seam open or to one side.

3. Continue stitching the strips together until you have one long continuous strip of binding.

4. Fold the strip lengthwise, wrong sides together and press.

5. Draw miter lines along each corner of the quilt. Beginning along one long edge on the quilt, pin the raw edges of the quilt binding to the edges of the right side of the quilt top.

6. Stitch using the seam allowance given in the specific instructions, starting about 1" (2.5cm) from the end of the strip. Stop stitching at the miter line and backstitch.

7. Fold a ¾" (2cm) pleat in the binding at the corner and begin stitching again along the second side of the binding, starting at the miter line (fig. 2).

8. Continue stitching, using the same technique at each corner. Stitch through all layers. Stop stitching about 2" (5cm) from the beginning. Overlap the beginning and the end ½" (1.3cm) and trim away any excess. Fold one edge of the binding to the inside ¼" (6mm). Place the straight end into the folded end and continue stitching (fig. 3).

9. Fold the binding over the edges of the quilt, enclosing the seam allowance. Place the folded edge of the binding just past the seam line. At the corner, the binding will fold into a miter. To stitch the binding in place by machine, use a straight stitch, or whipstitch it in place by hand (fig. 4).

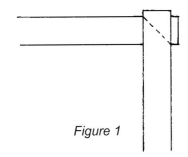

Figure 1

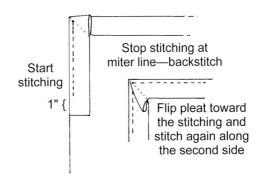

Start stitching

1" {

Stop stitching at miter line—backstitch

Flip pleat toward the stitching and stitch again along the second side

Figure 2

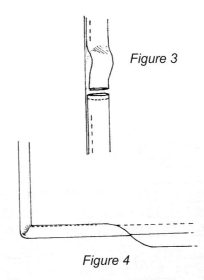

Figure 3

Figure 4

Sashing

NOTE: Illustrations show a nine-patch quilt top; the technique is the same for all sashed quilts, even though the number of blocks may be different. Refer to the specific instructions for each quilt.

1. Cut sashing strips to the dimensions stated in the specific quilt instructions. Some quilts will have short sashing strips on each side of each block, with a smaller square block at each intersection. Others will have short sashings in one direction and long strips in the other direction, making the smaller squares unnecessary.

2. Refer to specific quilt instructions for the size of all seam allowances. If blocks will be pieced into horizontal rows, attach a short sashing between the side edges of every two blocks (fig. 1a). There may also be a sashing on each outside edge of the completed row (fig. 1b); refer to the specific instructions. Press all seams toward the darker color if shadowing would show through on the lighter color; if shadowing is not a problem, press the seams toward the sashing.

3. If the blocks will be pieced into vertical columns, attach a short sashing between the top and bottom edges of every two blocks (fig. 2a). There may also be a sashing on top and bottom edges of the completed column (fig. 2b); refer to the specific instructions. Press all seams toward the darker color if shadowing would show through on the lighter color; if shadowing is not a problem, press the seams toward the sashing.

4. If short sashings will be used to piece the rows or columns, attach the small squares between the short ends of every two sashing pieces to create one long sashing strip for each column or row

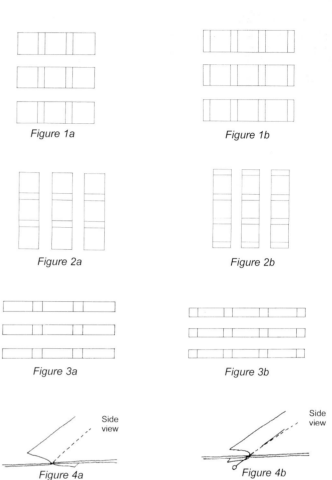

Figure 1a

Figure 1b

Figure 2a

Figure 2b

Figure 3a

Figure 3b

Figure 4a

Figure 4b

(fig. 3a). If the column or row has sashings on the outer edges, there will be a small square at the ends of the completed row or column (fig. 3b); refer to the specific instructions. Press all seams toward the darker color if shadowing would show through on the lighter color; if shadowing is not a problem, press the seams toward the small squares.

5. Piece the rows or columns with sashings between as before; refer to the specific instructions for each quilt. If there are small squares in the long sashings, be sure that the seams match exactly where they cross at intersections. If seams are pressed in opposite directions, slide the pieces together until the seams

butt together (fig. 4a). If the seams are pressed in the same direction, place a pin exactly through the stitching line of each seam to be sure that seams are exactly aligned (fig. 4b); remove the pin at the last possible moment before stitching over the seam.

6. Press the seams to one side as before. If shadowing is not a problem, press the seams toward the sashings.

7. Press the entire completed top, then proceed with construction as directed in the specific quilt instructions.

Stitch Glossary

Straight Stitch

Simply bring the needle up from under the fabric and insert it into the fabric a short distance in front of where the needle came up. It is an in-and-out stitch. Remember to pull the ribbon loosely for full stitches.

Figure 1   *Figure 2*

Lazy Daisy Stitch

1. Bring the needle up through the center point if you are stitching a flower, and up just next to a vine or flower for leaves (fig. 1).

2. Insert the needle into the same hole in which you came up. In the same stitch come through about ⅛" to ⅜" (3mm to 1cm) above that point (fig. 2). Wrap the ribbon behind the needle and pull the ribbon through, keeping the ribbon from twisting (fig. 3).

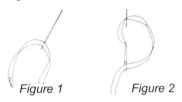

Figure 1   *Figure 2*

3. Insert the needle straight into the same hole or very close to the same hole at the top of the loop (fig. 4). Notice that the needle goes down underneath the ribbon loop (side view fig. 4). The top view of figure 4 shows that the stitch is straight and will anchor the ribbon loop in place.

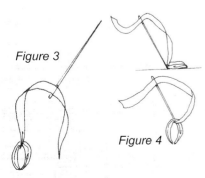

Figure 3

Figure 4

No-Fail French Knot

1. Bring the needle up through the fabric (fig. 1).

2. Hold the needle horizontally with one hand and wrap the ribbon around the needle with the other hand (fig. 2). If you are using a single strand of floss, one or two wraps will create a small knot. If you are making French knots with ¹⁄₁₆"(2mm) silk ribbon, the knot will be larger. The size of the knot varies with the number of strands of floss or the width of the silk ribbon being used.

3. While holding the tail of the ribbon to prevent it from unwinding off the needle, bring the needle up into a vertical position and insert it into the fabric just slightly beside where the needle came out of the fabric (fig. 3). Pull the ribbon or floss gently through the fabric while holding the tail with the other hand.

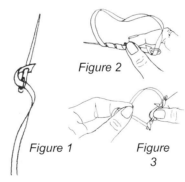

Figure 2

Figure 1   *Figure 3*

Japanese Ribbon Stitch

Bring the needle up from under the fabric, loop it around and insert the needle down into the center of the ribbon a short distance in front of where the needle came up. Pull the ribbon so that the end curls in on itself loosely so that it does not disappear.

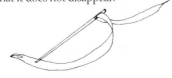

Stem/Outline Stitch

1. Come up from behind at A and go down into the fabric again at B (see fig. 1). This is a little below the line. Come back up at C (fig. 1). This is a little above the line. Keep the thread below the needle.

2. Go back down into the fabric at D and come up a little above the line at B (fig. 2).

3. Continue working, always keeping the thread below the needle (fig. 3).

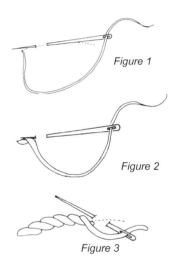

Figure 1

Figure 2

Figure 3

Satin Stitch

1. It generally helps if you have the area to be filled traced on the project so that you have two definite lines to guide and maintain the varying width of the stitch as it fills different shapes. Secure fabric in an embroidery hoop.

2. Begin at one end and work the needle from one side to the other, stacking the thread up just below and next to the previous stitch (fig. 1). Continue this wrapping process, keeping the fabric secured and taut while the stitches are pulled with light tension so that the fabric will not tunnel.

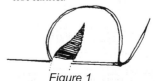

Figure 1

Important note: Templates have been reduced by 50%—
enlarge templates by 200% on a photocopier before using.

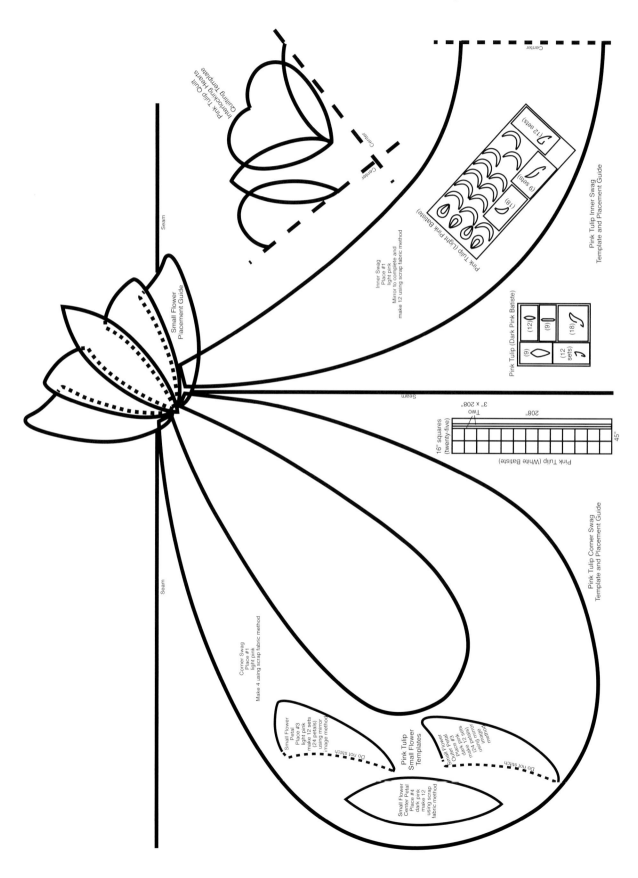

28

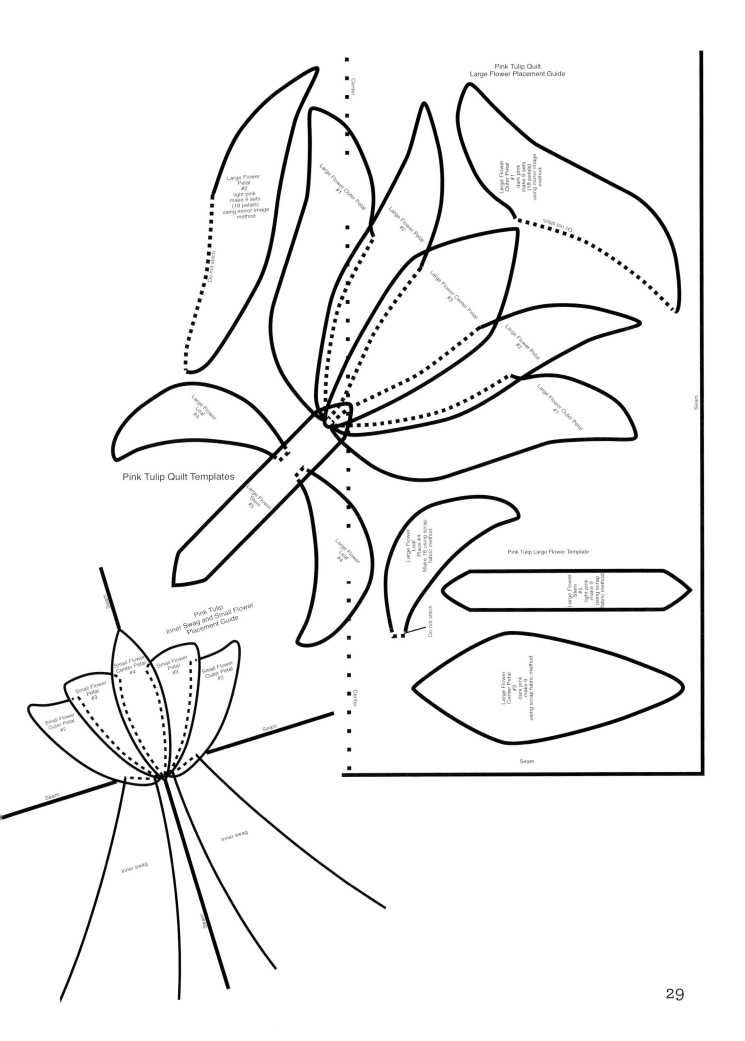

Pink Tulip Quilt
Large Flower Placement Guide

Center

Large Flower Petal #2
light pink
make 9 sets
(18 petals)
using mirror image method

Do not stitch

Large Flower Outer Petal #1

Large Flower Petal #2

Large Flower Center Petal #3

Large Flower Petal #2

Large Flower Outer Petal #1

Large Flower Outer Petal #2
dark pink
make 9 sets
(18 petals)
using mirror image method

Do not stitch

Seam

Large Flower Leaf #4

Large Flower Stem #5

Pink Tulip Quilt Templates

Large Flower Leaf #4

Large Flower Leaf #4
Place #4
Make 18 using scrap fabric method

Do not stitch

Pink Tulip Large Flower Template

Large Flower Stem #5
light pink
make 9
using scrap fabric method

Large Flower Center Petal #3
dark pink
make 9
using scrap fabric method

Pink Tulip
Inner Swag and Small Flower
Placement Guide

Small Flower Center Petal #4

Small Flower Petal #3

Small Flower Outer Petal #2

Small Flower Petal #3

Seam

Small Flower Outer Petal #2

Seam

Seam

Seam

Inner swag

Inner swag

Inner swag

29

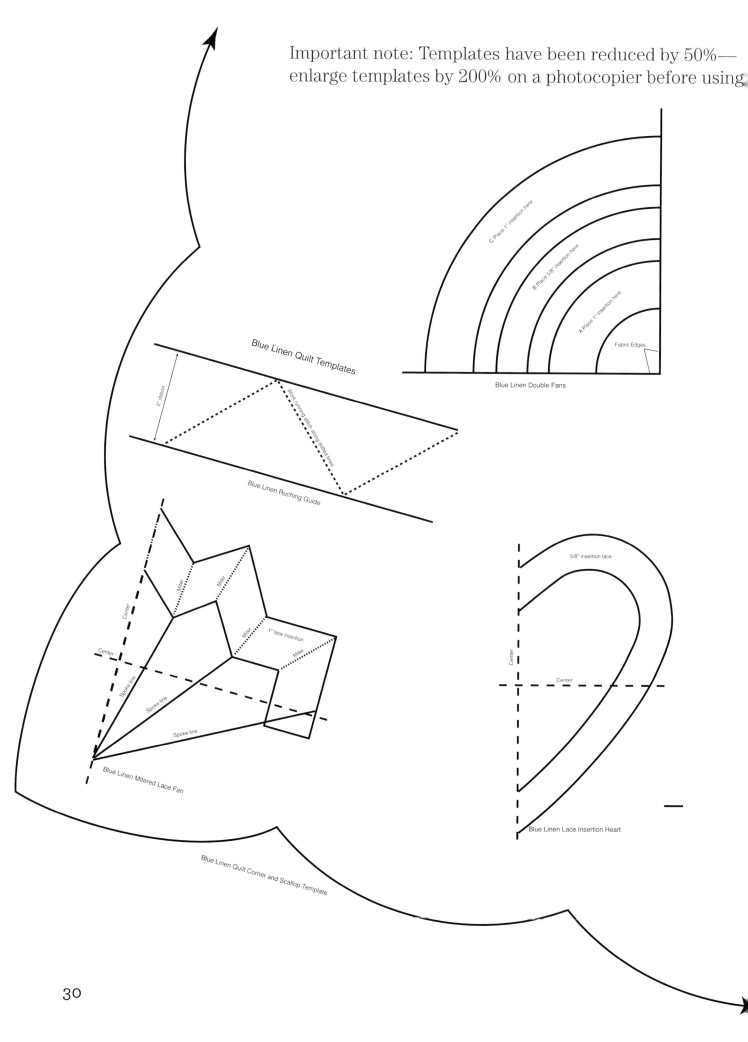

Important note: Templates have been reduced by 50%—
enlarge templates by 200% on a photocopier before using

Blue Linen Quilt Templates

C Place 1" insertion here

B Place 5/8" insertion here

A Place 1" insertion here

Fabric Edges

Blue Linen Double Fans

2" ribbon

Work running stitch along dotted lines

Blue Linen Ruching Guide

Center

Miter

Miter

Miter

1" lace insertion

Miter

Center

Spoke line

Spoke line

Spoke line

Blue Linen Mitered Lace Fan

5/8" insertion lace

Center

Center

Blue Linen Lace Insertion Heart

Blue Linen Quilt Corner and Scallop Template

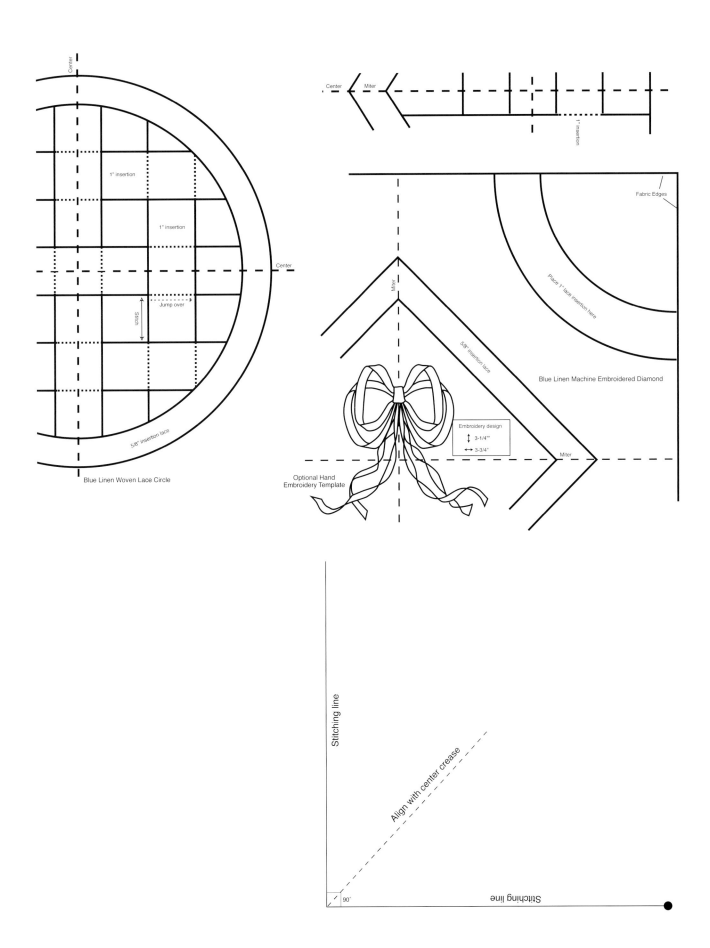

Center

Center

1" insertion

1" insertion

Stitch

Jump over

5/8" insertion lace

Blue Linen Woven Lace Circle

Center   Miter

1" insertion

Fabric Edges

Place 1" lace insertion here

Miter

5/8" insertion lace

Blue Linen Machine Embroidered Diamond

Miter

Embroidery design

3-1/4""

3-3/4"

Optional Hand
Embroidery Template

Stitching line

Align with center crease

90°

Stitching line

Settings for Entredeux and Pin Stitch

Bernina 180 E
Pin Stitch
- 100 wing needle or 100 universal
- Stitch no. 330 as is or L=2.5, W=2.5

Entredeux
- 100 wing or 100 universal
- Stitch no. 701 as is or L=2.5, W=3.0

Pfaff 2140
Pin Stitch
- 100 wing or 100 universal
- Stitch no. 139, tension 3, twin needle button, L=3, W=4

Entredeux
- 100 wing or 100 universal
- Stitch no. 142, L=2.5, W=4

Pfaff 7570
Pin Stitch
- 100 wing or 100 universal
- Stitch no. 112, tension 3, twin needle button, L=3, W=4

Entredeux
- 100 wing or 100 universal
- Stitch no. 132, L=5, W=3.5
- Stitch no. 113, L=2, W=4
- Stitch no. 114, L=2.5, W=3.5
- Stitch no. 115, L=3, W=3.5

Husqvarna Viking Designer I and 1+
Pin Stitch
- 100 wing needle or 100 universal
- Stitch no. D6, L=2.5–3, W=2–2.5

Entredeux
- 100 wing needle or 100 universal
- Stitch no. D7 (as is)

Elna Xquisit
Pin Stitch
- 100 wing needle or 100 universal
- Stitch 2/09, L=2.5, W=3

Entredeux
- 100 wing needle or 100 universal
- Stitch 2/10, L=1.5, W=5

Elna EnVision
Pin Stitch
- 100 wing needle or 100 universal
- Stitch 149, L=2.5, W=2.5

Entredeux
- 100 wing needle or 100 universal
- Stitch 36, L=1.5, W=2.5

Singer XL-5000
Pin Stitch
- 100 wing needle or 100 universal
- Screen no. 1, Stitch no. 7
- Medium or Small (width changes with length)

Entredeux
- 100 wing needle or 100 universal
- Screen no. 1, Stitch no. 8
- Medium or Small (width changes with length)

Singer XL-1000
Pin Stitch
- 100 wing needle or 100 universal
- Screen no. 6, Stitch no. 7
- Medium or Small (width changes with length)

Entredeux
- 100 wing needle or 100 universal
- Screen no. 6, Stitch no. 8
- Medium or Small (width changes with length)

Janome 10,000
Pin Stitch
- 100 wing needle or 100 universal
- Stitch no. 87 or 88, L=1.5 - 2.5, W=1.5-2.5

Entredeux
- 100 wing needle or 100 universal
- Stitch no. 97, L=1.0, W=3.5

Brother ULT 2001
Pin Stitch
- 100 wing needle or 100 universal
- Screen no. 3, Stitch no. 4, L=3.0, W=2.5

Entredeux
- 100 wing needle or 100 universal
- Screen no. 3, Stitch no. 8, L=2.5, W=3.0

Baby Lock Ellagéo
Choose Decorative Stitch
Heirloom Pin stitch
- 100 wing needle or 100 universal
- Stitch 3/04 , L=2.5, W=3.5

Entredeux
- 100 wing needle or 100 universal
- Stitch 3/08, L=3.5, W=5

Baby Lock Esanté
Choose Decorative Stitch
Heirloom Pin Stitch
- 100 wing needle or 100 universal
- Stitch no. 4 (as is)

Entredeux
- 100 wing needle or 100 universal
- Stitch no. 5 (as is)